Credit Secrets

Learn the concepts of Credit Scores, How to Boost them and Take Advantages from Your Credit Cards

PIERCE LOWE

The trademarks that are used are without any consent, and the publication of the trademark is without permission or backing by the trademark owner. All trademarks and brands within this book are for clarifying purposes only and are the owned by the owners themselves, not affiliated with this document

Contents

Introduction

A credit card can assist you in establishing credit, making accessible payments, and meeting day-to-day expenses. Understanding how credit cards work can help you understand the advantages of having one as compared to having a debit card. Understanding how credit cards work can help you manage your debt more responsibly. Credit cards provide you with a line of credit that you can use to make balance transfers, purchases, and/or cash advances while also requiring you to repay the loan amount over time. When paying with a credit card, you must make the minimum payment each month by the balance's due date. Interest will be charged if they do not pay the full balance for purchases. For balance transfers or cash advances, interest will be charged from the date of the transaction. A yearly fee or an introductory annual fee may be charged on credit cards. The fee amount varies by card and is subject to change after an introductory offer. You may also be charged a late fee if you make a late payment. Depending on the activity, some credit cards may also charge additional fees. Cash advance fees, balance transfer fees and foreign transaction fees are just a few examples. Credit cards, unlike debit cards, can be used to raise your credit score. Each monthly payment you make will be reported to the 3 credit reporting agencies by your credit card issuer. You can contribute to the successful rating of the credit score with each monthly bill that you pay. Using credit cards wisely on a regular basis helps you build credit by demonstrating to lenders that you can handle debt. A credit card can help you manage your finances. Making on-time credit card payments will help you pay off the debt and improve the credit score by lowering your credit-to-debt ratio. Making the least minimum monthly payment on or before the deadline is critical for managing your monthly credit card bill. A secured credit card requires a security deposit, which is held in an interest-bearing U.S. savings account. Under your name, open a bank-backed savings account. Your application will be reviewed after you submit the deposit, and if approved, you would be sent a card with a credit line equal to the amount of your deposit. Your monthly payments would still be reported to the 3 major credit bureaus each month, so staying current is critical to maintaining a good credit score. Your cumulative financial health depends on your credit score. You may face difficulties obtaining favorable terms on a variety of loans if you don't have a good credit score, such as for a new car, a home, or education. Your credit score is a way for lenders to determine whether or not to give you a loan, a credit card, rent you a flat, or even set up cable, phone, or water service in a new home based on your financial responsibility. Your credit score can be improved, and you should learn how to keep it up. Your credit behavior is heavily weighted in the calculation of your credit score. You can improve the credit history by using credit cards responsibly. "Responsible" is the key word here. Keep your spending under control and, at the same time, ensure that your credit limit does not exceed your savings account balance. Consider applying for only two credit cards: a store credit card and the main credit card. Make small purchases with these cards and pay off the balances in full each month. As you will read this book, you will develop a good understanding of the benefits of credit and the different myths related to credit.

CHAPTER 1: What are Credit Reports and Credit Scores?

In this chapter, you will learn about the fundamentals of credit reports and credit scores and how to secure a copy of your credit report and correct any mistakes in it. Doing this will support you enhance your credit score.

Credit reports

Your current debt, payment history, loans and other financial information are all listed on your credit report. They reveal where you live and work, as well as whether you've been arrested, sued or declared bankrupt. A credit report is a document that contains details about your credit history and current credit situation, such as loan repayment history and credit account status. The majority of people have multiple credit reports. Credit reporting companies which are also called credit bureaus or consumer reporting agencies, collect and process financial information about you that creditors, like lenders, credit card companies, and other financial institutions, submit to them. Creditors aren't obligated to report to all credit reporting agencies.

Various uses of credit reports

Lenders use credit reports to determine whether or not to extend your credit as well as accept a loan. The reports also aid in determining the interest rate you will be charged. Your credit report may be examined by potential insurers, employers, and landlords. You won't even know whether the credit report will be used to check the credit by a creditor or an employer. Your credit reports are collected and maintained by credit reporting agencies (CRAs). Each CRA keeps its own data and may not have all of your accounts' information. Despite the fact that their reports differ, no one agency is more essential than the others. And the data that every agency has should be correct. Credit reports are used by lenders to determine whether or not they will lend you money and what interest rates they would then offer you. Your credit report is also used by lenders to see if you are still meeting the terms of even an existing credit account. Other companies may use your credit reports to decide whether or not to offer you insurance, rent you a home or apartment, or provide you with cable TV, internet, utility as well as cell phone service. Your credit report may be used to make employment decisions if you concur to let an employer look at it. The following information is frequently found on credit reports:

Personal information

- Any name, including your name that you may have used in the past in relation to a credit account. This includes even nicknames
- Present and past addresses
- Your birth date

- Social Security number
- Phone numbers

Credit accounts

- Present and historical credit accounts. These also include the type of account such as installment, mortgage, revolving, etc.)
- Your credit limit or amount
- Your account balance
- The payment history of your account
- The account opening and closing date
- The name of the creditor

Collection items Public records

- **Bankruptcies**
- Civil suits and **judgments**
- Liens
- **Foreclosures**

A credit report may include information on long due child support from a state or local child support agency, as well as information from any local, state, as well as the federal government agency.

Reasons for checking your credit report

Verify your credit reports on a regular basis to ensure that your financial and personal information is correct. It also

ensures that no fraudulent accounts have been opened in your name. Take action to correct any errors you find on your credit report.

Learn methods to verify your credit report

You can get a free yearly credit report from each of the 3 credit reporting organizations at AnnualCreditReport.com. Experian, Equifax, and TransUnion are among these companies. Many cities are having financial difficulties as a result of unpredictable and troubling economic conditions. You could get free credit reports each week until April 2022 to stay in control of your finances. You can order all 3 reports all together or one by one. Find out when you can get a free credit report in other situations.

Credit Scores

A credit score is typically a figure that indicates how likely you are to default on your debt. It can assist creditors in determining whether or not to extend credit to you, as well as the terms and interest rate they offer. A good score can help you in a variety of ways. It may make getting a loan, renting a residence, or lowering your insurance value easier. Your credit score is calculated using information from your credit report. It is based on the following:

- Payment history
- New credit accounts' applications
- Exceptional balances
- Kinds of credit accounts such as car loans, credit cards, car loans
- Size of credit history

It's critical to ensure that the credit story is correct so that the credit score could be accurate as well. It is possible to have several credit scores. They aren't computed by similar credit reporting organizations which keep track of your credit. Instead, they're made of various businesses or lenders, each with their very own credit scoring scheme.

Your credit score is not included in the free annual credit report, but you can get it from a variety of places. It's possible that the credit card agency will provide it to you for free. One of the 3 main credit reporting organizations may also sell it to you. When you get your score, you usually get some advice on how to improve it.

Credit Freeze

You can limit access to the credit report by placing a credit freeze. This is critical following a data breach as well as identity theft when your own information could be used to open new credit accounts. Prior to opening the other account, most creditors check your credit report. Creditors cannot access your credit report if it's frozen, so they're unlikely to approve illegal applications. You have the freedom to place or remove a credit freeze at any time. You can put a freeze on personal credit files as well as your children's credit files if they are 15 or younger.

Credit freeze

To put a freeze on your credit report, contact each credit reporting agency. Freeze requests can be submitted online, over a call, or by mail to each agency.

Lift a Credit Freeze

You must either lift your credit freeze temporarily or permanently if you really want lenders as well as other firms to have access to your credit files once again. Make contact with each credit bureau. To raise your credit freeze, you'll need a password or PIN. You are free to raise your credit freeze as much as you want to. When you request a lift online or over the phone, it takes sixty minutes for it to be processed. If you ask for the lift by mail, it may take up to 3 business days.

Errors on Your Credit Report

If you discover inaccuracies on the credit report, compose a letter debating the inaccuracy and attach any supporting documentation. Now, send it to:

- The credit reporting agency (Experian, Equifax, or TransUnion)

- The data provider provided the credit reporting agency with inaccurate information. Credit card firms and banks are examples of these providers.

Your credit report must be corrected by the credit reporting agency (CRA) and the data provider. This would include any inaccuracies or gaps in the data. The Fair Credit Reporting Act mandates that any errors be corrected. You can lodge an objection with the Consumer Financial Protection Bureau if your written dispute does not result in the correction of the error (CFPB).

Negative Data in a Credit Report

Public records such as judgments, tax liens, and bankruptcies are examples of negative information on a credit report that gives a vision of your financial status and debts. Most negative data can be reported for 7 years by a credit reporting agency. You can report data about a lawsuit or even a verdict against you for 7 years and until the statute of limits expires, whichever comes first. Bankruptcies can stay on your record for up to ten years, and tax liens that are unpaid can stay on your record for up to fifteen years.

Correcting Mistakes in a Credit Report

Anybody who refuses to give you housing, credit, a job or insurance because of a credit report should provide you with the address, name, and phone number of the credit reporting agency (CRA) which generated the report. If a company denies you credit based on your credit report, you have the right to demand a free report within sixty days under the Fair Credit Reporting Act (FCRA). If your credit report includes incomplete or inaccurate information, you can have it corrected:

- Contact the credit reporting agency as well as the company which provided the CRA with the information.

- Inform the CRA in writing of any information that you think is incorrect. Make a copy of everything you send and receive.

Some businesses may pledge to repair as well as fix your credit for a fee up front, but there is no other way to eliminate inaccurate negative information from your credit report.

Make a Complaint

You can make a complaint with the Consumer Financial Protection Bureau if you have a problem with credit reporting (CFPB).

Medical History Report

A medical history report is a list of your current and previous medical conditions. These reports are used by insurance companies to determine whether or not to offer you coverage. MIB, the organization that handles and keeps the reporting database, has the right to send you a copy of your report.

Information Sources for a Medical History Report

If you disclosed a medical situation on an insurance request, the insurer might be required to notify MIB. Only if you give written permission can an insurer share the medical condition with MIB. The condition will be involved in the medical history report if you give permission. The complete medical records are not included in your medical history report. MIB does not accept information from hospitals, doctors, pharmacies, or other health experts. The report will not include a complete list of your diagnoses, blood tests, or medications. For seven years, a bit of information remains on your report. Only when you ask for an insurance program with a MIB-member company and provide them approval to submit the medical conditions to MIB can your report be updated.

Learn the way the insurers make use of medical history reports

The insurer may request approval to review the medical history report when you apply for insurance. Your report can only be accessed by an insurance company if you allow them. The data you provided in previous insurance applications are included in the report. These reports are read by insurers before they grant applications for:

- Health
- Life
- Long-term
- Disability insurance applications or
- Critical illness

You can make a request for your free medical history report

Each year, you are entitled to receive one free copy of the medical history report, which is also called your MIB consumer file. You can get a copy of the following documents:

- Yourself

- The minor child

- Someone, as a rightful guardian

- Someone, as a representative under a power of attorney

A medical history report is not available to everyone. If you haven't applied for insurance in the last 7 years, the insurance policy is through an employer policy or a group, the insurance company isn't a member of MIB, or you didn't provide an insurer approval to submit the medical reports to MIB, you won't have a report.

Medical ID Scams and Reports

To see if you've been a target of medical ID robbery, look at your medical history report. If there is a report on your name, but you've not requested insurance in the last 7 years, you could be a victim. If the report includes ill-health, which you don't have, this is another indication of medical ID theft.

File a Complaint

Examine your report to ensure that it only contains information about medical conditions which you have. If your report is not correct, request a re-investigation.

CHAPTER 2: The Advantages of Having a Credit Card

Paying with a credit card may provide you with valuable benefits that you would not be able to obtain using other methods. Credit cards have an added benefit over other payment methods because they allow you to earn rewards through purchases. If you can commit to spending only what you can pay off in full each month, paying for your purchases with a credit card can bring numerous advantages. Many of the benefits that credit cards offer can actually save you money over the long term. Credit can be a useful tool for improving your finances, gaining access to the best financial products, saving money on interest, and even avoiding the need to put down a deposit when opening utility and/or cell phone accounts. A nice credit score and a good credit report have numerous advantages. While some people have had bad experiences with credit in the past, it can be a very valuable asset when used responsibly. Continue reading to learn about the benefits of using credit, as we've compiled a list of some of the common benefits of having a credit card.

Pay for purchases over time

Credit cards allow you to pay for something today with your card and pay off the balance later. Most issuers provide a grace period during which you are not required to pay interest. This grace period usually lasts from the time you make your purchase until the end of the billing cycle in which it was made, and it ends when the payment is due. However, unless you're taking advantage of a promotional 0% annual percentage rate offer, if you have a balance on your credit card, you'll normally have to pay interest on the balance owed.

Convenience

Managing your finances with a credit card is more convenient than with another payment method. Each month, your credit card issuer sends you a statement with the details regarding when, where, and how much you spent on all purchases made with your card. You can keep track of your spending using the information from these statements. Furthermore, some credit cards provide year-end statements which summarize spending over the course of the year, which is useful for tax purposes and other monitoring purposes. Because you won't be paying for online purchases with cash, credit cards are a convenient way to pay. The debit card and/or bank account information is not at risk when you use a credit card.

Save on interest and fees

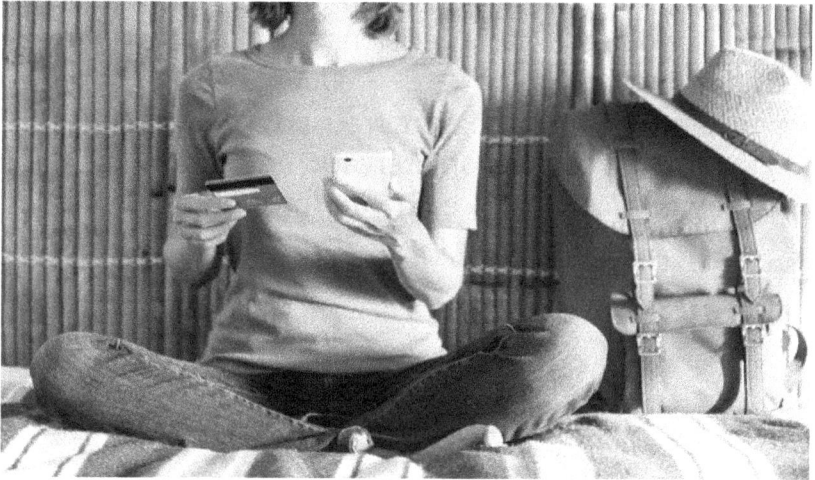

The most significant advantage of having good to excellent credit is the ability to save money. When it comes to buying a home, for instance, having good credit can save you tens of thousands of dollars, especially on a mortgage loan. People with better credit typically get lower interest rates on credit cards, private student loans, auto loans, personal loans, and lines of credit. If you plan to buy a house with a mortgage sometime in the future, your credit score may play a role in determining how much you can afford and whether you can buy a house at all. However, saving money on interest is one of the many advantages of having a good credit score.

Manage your cash flow

You don't have to pay for a new purchase right away if you use a credit card. When you usually swipe your card, the bank holds the funds until you pay it back. You won't have to pay any interest on such purchases if you pay off the entire balance by the statement due date, which is a good habit to develop. As a result, make sure you pay your

credit card bills on time. You need to learn more about how to make good credit card decisions. You have till your next statement final payment date + about 3 weeks before you have to pay up from the date you buy the purchase. This could mean 3 to 7 weeks of interest-free borrowing, allowing you to pay off your balance on your own time.

Avoid utility deposits

During the onboarding process for a new cell phone account or moving into a new home and setting up utility services, the provider would most likely check your credit. If the score falls below the company's minimum requirements, you'll be required to make a cash deposit in order to open an account. The additional startup costs of utility deposits along with moving costs could be financially challenging in a country where 78 percent of people live paycheck to paycheck. Having a good credit history could even help you keep the money in your bank account rather than with the utility company.

Emergency fund backup plan

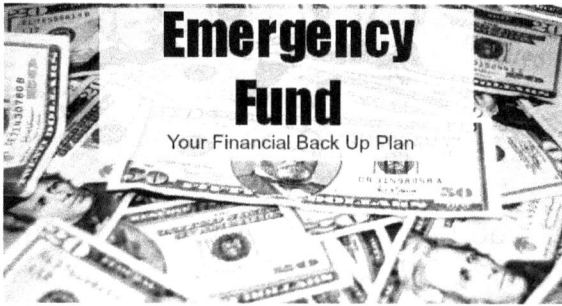

A recent Federal Reserve report confirmed a long-held statistic that forty percent of Americans could not afford to pay for a $400 emergency out of their savings. It's a positive thing they have credit as a backup plan because the average home repair, car repair or medical bill could really easily be multiple times that $400 figure. If you're self-employed, you should have an emergency fund that can cover at least 3 to 6 months' worth of expenses. Even the most prepared individuals should be aware that they have access to additional funds through lines of credit, credit cards and other borrowing options, if necessary.

Travel benefits

The credit card may have a range of attributes that could

really help you save money on your next trip. Auto rental collision damage waivers, baggage delay insurance, trip delay reimbursement, a free checked bag, trip cancellation as well as interruption insurance, insurance, free airport lounge access, travel statement credits, and other travel benefits are examples of these benefits. If you rent cars frequently, collision damage waiver coverage is among the benefits that you may find yourself using frequently. When you do not accept the rental company's collision insurance as well as charge the car rental to a card that offers the coverage, this waiver usually kicks in. Depending on the benefits of your card, it may provide primary coverage, in which case it pays out first or secondary coverage, in which case it pays out after you've filed a claim with your insurance company. In either case, you'll avoid having to pay for the insurance provided by the rental car company. Certain credit cards have benefits that can help you save money on flights. For instance, airline credit cards could include perks such as a free checked bag or access to the airline's sitting rooms. Some credit cards even give you a travel statement credit to help you pay for things like airline fees. Many travel benefits can come in handy in the event of misplaced luggage or trips that are delayed or canceled. These benefits may be able to cover all or some of your additional costs.

Purchase and travel protections

Many of the greatest credit cards automatically insure your purchases. You can use price change protection, purchase protection, extended warranty coverage and other benefits offered by some credit cards instead of paying for expensive retailer purchase coverage. When traveling, credit cards can provide rental car insurance, trip accident or delay insurance, lost or delayed baggage insurance, as well as other unique and productive benefits that can save you a lot of money and time if something goes wrong.

Don't underestimate the power of good credit

If you use your credit wisely, you can save tens of thousands of dollars. Poor credit management, on the other hand, could even rapidly escalate into a costly and complex effort. That is why you should read the credit report as well as credit score carefully. The good news is that you can build the credit over time to get access to the credit accounts that you want in the future, even if you have bad credit right now. Take the time to learn how to manage your credit, and you'll reap the benefits for decades.

Better credit card rewards

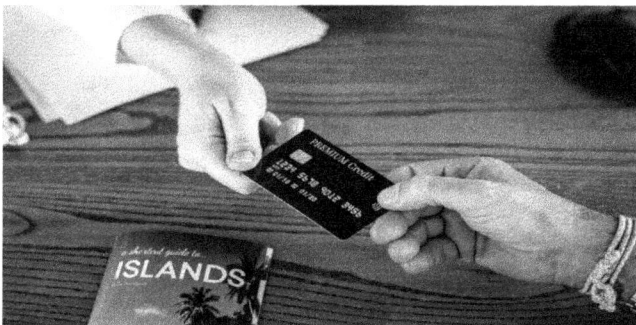

One of the most obvious benefits of having a credit card is

the way to earn rewards for your purchases. For earning, managing, and redeeming rewards, almost every rewards program has its own system. A rewards card that offers miles as well as points that could be used toward flights as well as hotel rooms could be very useful for frequent travelers. A credit card that offers cash back as a statement credit, direct deposit, or even a check may be a better option for those who prefer cash. Your rewards could even cover the cost of an entire vacation, based on your spending habits. To persuade you to apply for and use a credit card, many companies offer sign-up bonuses. These bonuses can be worth up to $500. It's easy to see how you could cover a vacation by combining the everyday rewards with a bunch of sign-up bonuses. When you pay with cash or debit, you'll get nothing but the service or product you paid for. A cash back or travel rewards credit card, on the other hand, will give you 1% to 5% back on every purchase, which you can deposit in your bank account, use to reduce your balance with statement credits or use to cover the cost of an upcoming flight as well as a hotel stay. You won't be able to get some of the best rewards credit cards as well as credit card offers if you have bad credit. Only a small number of credit cards designed for people with bad or limited credit offer any type of reward. However, as your credit improves into the good overall ranges, you'll be able to take advantage of some fantastic rewards for purchases you've already made.

Fraud protection

The liability for credit card fraud is limited to $50 under federal law. You are not liable for any fraud if you notify your card issuer that you have lost your card well before fraudulent charges are made or if the card information (and not the actual card) is stolen. Many credit card companies go even further and don't hold you liable for fraud if you report unauthorized charges promptly. Your credit card issuer may provide virtual account numbers that you can use when making purchases over the phone or online to help make the credit card even more secure. This ensures that the primary credit card number isn't compromised in the event of a data breach. If you use your debit card and your card number is stolen at a gas station, restaurant, as well as online, the cybercriminal has access to your checking account and can drain all of your funds. This can leave you unable to pay your rent or mortgage, as well as leave you without enough money to eat, and this can take months to get your money back, if at all. Credit card fraud liability is more highly restricted than debit card fraud liability. If an unauthorized purchase is made on your credit card, simply notify the issuer, and the charge will be removed from your statement. Most credit cards have no liability for fraudulent transactions and offer more fraud protection options.

Free credit scores

As a perk, several credit cards now provide free credit scores. Your credit score may be printed on the monthly statements by some credit card companies. Others provide a free credit score program or the ability to view your credit score on the bank's website. A credit card benefit that allows you to check your credit score does not qualify as a hard inquiry and does not affect your credit score. When looking at the free credit score, ensure that you know what kind of score you've received. You won't be able to see your FICO score on all cards, which is the most popularly used credit scoring model among lenders. Some credit cards allow you to see your VantageScore rather than your FICO score. Free credit scores, on the other hand, can help you see whether your credit score is getting better or declining over time.

Price protection

Have you ever purchased something only to find out that the price had dropped just a few days later? If you made the purchase on a card that gives price protection, it might be able to assist you. Within certain guidelines, price protection will usually refund the difference between the price you actually paid and now the lower price. Whilst price protection has recently been removed from many credit cards; it is still available on a few. The programs have limitations. Price drops usually last a few months, and you may be required to furnish an advertisement displaying the lower price in order to receive a refund. The amount you could save per purchase is usually limited to around $250, and the benefit has a yearly cap on how much you could save. Certain purchases are also not permitted.

Purchase protection

Purchase protection protects products that have been purchased with an eligible credit card from damage or theft. These benefits typically cover new purchases for three months after purchase, but this can vary depending on the card issuer. There are also prohibitions that you need to be concerned about, such as animals, all types of tickets, boats, cars, and planes, refurbished items, and so on. Specifics can be found in the benefit guide that came with your card. Your credit card benefit may repair or pay back for the purchase amount up to a limit, like $1,000, if your item is damaged or stolen. Aside from per-item caps, the total sum of claims you can make in a year may be limited. Although you may choose to use a card that gives you the most points per dollar for each purchase, it is prudent to use the card that provides the best purchase protection when purchasing a high-end item.

Return protection

Return policies vary by retailer. Your credit card's return protection may allow you to return an item for a refund even if the retailer does not allow it. The benefit usually lasts for 3 months after you make a purchase, and you should make the purchase with the credit card that offers the benefit. This benefit's value may be restricted to a set amount per item, like $300, or a set amount per year, like $1,000. Furniture, appliances, and jewelry, for example, are typically not eligible for this benefit.

Extended warranty coverage

If you're buying an expensive item with a manufacturer's warranty, it's usually a good idea to use a credit card with extended warranty coverage to secure your investment. If your item breaks outside of the manufacturer's warranty and before the extended warranty expires, an extended warranty can reimburse you or get it repaired or replaced. Extended warranty rates differ by the card issuer. However, they typically add 1 or 2 years to a manufacturer's warranty. The maximum combined warranty, which includes both the manufacturers and extended warranties, is typically restricted to a certain number of years, like seven, and is likely capped in terms of a dollar amount. Extended warranty coverage, as with most credit card benefits, has its own set of limitations. It

doesn't extend to purchases that don't come with a warranty

from the manufacturer. Automobiles, boats, planes, and other motorized vehicles, for example, do not qualify. You must provide documentation to qualify for the benefit, which may include your purchase receipt as well as the main manufacturer's warranty. If you think you'll need the benefit in the future, keep this paperwork.

Make Sure You Have a Handle on Your Card and Its Benefits

Benefits programs for credit cards vary by issuer and even from credit card to credit card. The terms and conditions of these programs are usually spelled out in the credit card's benefits guide. This usually arrives at the same time as your card. You can also usually download it from the website of your credit card. Card issuers could even change these benefits at any time, and they usually come with a lot of rules and exclusions, so it's crucial to learn about the card's positive features before you use them. Whilst secondary credit card advantages can be beneficial; it's critical to keep the big picture in mind. If you carry a balance on your credit card and pay interest each month, the benefits of having one can be greatly reduced. Make sure that earning these secondary benefits with a credit card does not cost you more in fees and interest as compared to the value of the benefits you receive.

CHAPTER 3: Techniques for Improving Credit Scores

If you checked your credit reports and found your credit scores are not right where you figured they should be, you are not alone. Since your credit scores derive from details from your credit history, your financial performance offers a constantly maintained record about how careful you are with the credit you are utilizing. You will take care of your credit in different forms and thus control your financial future. The tips for optimizing your credit scores are given below:

Importance of choices on improving the credit score

Your credit score—a 3-digit number investors use to help them choose how likely it is they'll be paid on time if they give you a credit card or loan—is an important factor in your financial life. The better your grades, the more likely you are eligible for loans and credit cards at the most satisfactory terms, which will save you money. Your credit score — the usage of a three-digit rating by lenders to help them determine how easily they can be returned on time if they offer you a credit card or loan — has a big influence on your financial life. The better the scores, the more likely you would be to qualify at the most attractive rates for loans and credit cards which would save you money. You're not alone if your credit score isn't where you want it to be. It takes time to increase your credit scores, so the earlier you fix the problems that might pull them down, the earlier your credit scores can go up. You will improve your scores by taking multiple steps, such as keeping up a consistent record of paying bills on time, paying down debt and taking advantage of resources that allow you to attach bills for electricity and mobile phones to your credit sheet. We will explore and know about the role of different factors in your credit score to assist you in managing and sustaining excellent credit scores.

A look into the methods employed for credit scores' calculation

You probably have dozens of credit scores, if not hundreds. That's how a credit score is determined by adding a statistical formula to the details in one of the three credit reports because there's no specific standardized method utilized by all lenders or other finance institutions to determine the scores. It is necessary to remember that certain credit scoring models, such as the FICO ® Ranking, varying from 300 to 850, are very popular. However, you don't have to get stuck about having several scores since, typically, the reasons that make the ratings go up or down in various scoring models are identical. "What makes one score go up vs. down will still be the same — it depends on the degree. Many scoring models take your spending background on advances and credit cards into consideration, how much available credit you currently use, how long you have open balances, the kinds of balances you have and how much you ask for new credit.

Ways to significantly enhance the credit scores

Start by reviewing your credit reports online if you want to boost your scores. You can also get details regarding which variables influence your results the most when you get your scores. Such risk factors can allow you to realize the improvements you should make to continue your scores improving. You may need to give enough time for your creditors to notice any adjustments you create and then represent them in your credit scores. Some element in credit score is usually more critical than others, of course. For certain crucial credit scoring models, payment background and credit utilization ratios are probably the most relevant and combined, they can constitute up to 70% of a credit score, which implies they're highly significant.

Focusing on the acts below will further increase the credit scores over time. A credit score represents the trends of loan purchases over time, with a stronger focus on recent records.

Make it a habit to pay bills on time

As they check your credit report and query you for a credit score, they are really involved in how well you are paying the bills. That is since previous success in payments is generally deemed a strong indicator of potential results. This credit score aspect will be favorably affected by paying all the expenses on time, as decided each month. Paid late or resolving an account for less than you first decided to pay will have a detrimental effect on credit scores. You're going to have to pay your payments on time — not only credit card expenses or other debts you might have, such as vehicle loans or student loans but even the mortgage, insurance, mobile payments etc. It's always a smart idea to use the available services and devices, such as automated transfers or calendar alerts, to help ensure you pay on time per month. When you're late on some bills, get them up to date as quickly as possible. Although late or missing payments appear as negative facts on your seven-year credit report, their effect on your credit score decreases with time. Older late payments affect less than more recent ones.

Improve your credit by making your cell phone and utility payments on time

If you have made payments on time for the service and mobile phone, you will boost your credit score by factoring in certain payments. You will link to bank accounts to recognize a history of payment through service and telecom. Once the details are checked, the same is applied to the credit file. It will assist you with the final upgrading of the FICO ® rating.

Improve your credit by paying off debt and keeping balances at a minimum on credit cards and revolving credit

The significant statistic for determining credit score is the credit utilization ratio. It is determined by combining all of your credit card balances at any given time and dividing your total credit limit by that number. For example, if you normally spend around $2,000 a month and your overall credit limit is $10,000 across all your cards, then your use ratio is 20%. Check at all of the credit card receipts over the last twelve months to work out the total credit utilization ratio. For each month, apply the payment balances from all of your cards and divide them by twelve. This will give the average sum of credit you use per month.

Usually, lenders want to see small 30 percent or fewer percentages, so those with the highest credit scores also have very minimal credit utilization ratios. A low credit usage ratio shows lenders that you have not maxed out your credit cards and that you actually know how to handle credit well. You will affect the credit utilization ratio favorably by:

• Credit payments and small credit card balances.

• Becoming an authorized consumer on account of another party as long as they use the credit responsibly

You should open new credit accounts only as needed if you want to improve your credit score

You should not be tempted to open accounts for a better credit mix—it is not likely to boost your credit score. Unnecessary credit can impact your credit score negatively in multiple ways, from creating multiple hard inquiries on your credit report to luring you to indulge in splurge and debt.

Never close new credit cards

Holding unused credit cards open – as long as they don't cost you money in annual fees – is recommended as the best smart strategy, as shutting an account can improve your credit usage ratio. If you owe the same amount with fewer open accounts, it might lower your credit scores.

Keep yourself away from excessive new credit

This could contribute to several inquiries. That is because you will increase the maximum credit cap by obtaining a new credit card, but the process of applying for credit generates a tough inquiry on the credit report. Too many hard inquiries will adversely affect your credit score, but this influence may diminish with time. It is for two years that tough inquiries sit in the account sheet.

Keep a look for inaccuracies on the credit reports

Again, for three credit reporting bureaus, including TransUnion, Equifax, and Experian, you should search your credit reports for any inaccuracies. Faulty details on your credit reports could drag down your scores. Verify that the records indicated in the files are reliable. When you find mistakes, challenge the details and get them corrected instantly. Daily tracking of your credit will help you find inaccuracies before they can do any harm.

Time required for rebuilding your credit score

You should pay your bills and wait if you have negative facts regarding your credit score, such as late fees, a public record document, for example, unemployment, so many inquiries. Time is your partner in getting your credit scores higher. Poor credit scores don't have quick fixes. After a negative shift, the amount of time it takes to restore your credit score depends on the factors behind the change. Most of the unfavorable adjustments in credit scores were attributed to introducing a negative item, such as a delinquency or fraud record, to the credit report. Such new elements can begin to affect the credit ratings after a certain level is hit.

- Delinquencies last seven years on the credit sheet
- Some of the public record issues continue for seven years on the credit sheet, while certain bankruptcies can stay for 10 years
- Inquiries remain on your account for two years

It requires time to restore your credit and boost your credit scores, and there are no shortcuts. Begin strengthening your credit by checking details on your FICO ® Score and evaluating the specific variables that influence your credit scores. Next, read more about credit creation to boost your scores. And if you need assistance with your past payment mistakes, you should know something about fixing the account and how to restore the score.

Ways to build credit scores

When you do not have a credit report, you possibly have a slim credit sheet. The primary reason for that is because you have little financial knowledge or background. This assumes you have a few (if any) credit accounts, usually one to four, listed on your credit reports. For a fact, a thin file indicates a bank or insurer could not calculate a credit score since the financial report of a person does not provide adequate records to do so. There are activities you can do to fatten up your slim credit file, such as filing for a guaranteed credit card, being an approved recipient of someone else's credit card, or taking out a loan from a creditor.

You can improve credit history by using secured credit cards

Using secured credit cards can be a great way to build a credit history, or in your case, rebuild it. However, one significant warning is to make sure you register through a trustworthy company. Beware of the offers online that seem too sweet to be real. It might be a good place to start applying at the bank with which you have a checking account. To open a secured credit card account, a minimum amount of money has to be deposited into a bank account. The lender points out how much is required. You will then bill at the account up to a certain percentage of the total. That money is what keeps the account "secured." If you don't pay the bill, the lender will automatically deduct the funds from the payment account. You don't want to let that happen because it would show the bank you are not vigilant

in making the credit payments on time. The lender will ultimately turn the account into a regular, unsecured credit card account if you handle the protected account well, make payments and pay the bill on time per month. Ask your lender before opening a secured credit card account if he reports the account. Quite a few may not. It won't help you develop a financial background if they don't. However, when transferring it to a regular credit card account, the issuer may continue recording the transaction, and even though the protected card is not disclosed originally, this could be a way to get the foot in the door.

Impact of changes on scores

One important issue involves knowing whether a credit report can be impacted by specific actions. Closing two of your revolving accounts, for example, will increase your credit score. While this problem may seem simple to address, there are several considerations that need to be weighed.

- Credit ratings are focused solely on an individual's credit report records
- Any change to the credit report may impact the credit score of the person

Closing two accounts simply lower not only the number of opened revolving accounts but also lowers the total amount of available credit. This results in a higher consumption rate, which is often called the balance-to-limit ratio, because it usually reduces scores. One adjustment on a credit report will impact all of the items. It is difficult to give a totally objective estimation of how one single behavior would impact the credit score of an individual. This is why it is critical to have credit risk factors associated with your score. You determine which factors are having the biggest effect on your credit profile, and you can take corrective steps.

Critical Factors about credit scores

Credit scoring requires complicated equations, and the better you learn how credit reports and credit scores operate, the more you are able to take control of your own debts. Besides understanding the most significant variables found in credit scoring, learning a number of other details regarding credit reports and credit scores can be beneficial. These components are believed to be very important:

Negative information

Negative credit reporting facts will actually reduce the credit scores. The record persists for a specified amount of time on your credit card. Late fees, for example, appear for seven years after the day you missed a payment first. Paying off a fraud account won't erase it from the credit history automatically. Depending on the type of insolvency, bankruptcies can remain on your report for seven to ten years. The positive thing is that, finally, any unfavorable

thing will run off the credit report. Focus on the stuff you should better influence, like paying all of the expenses on time, before it happens.

Monthly Credit Balance

To build your credit history, you do not need to carry a monthly credit card balance. Each month you should settle your credit card debts and have a good impact on your credit rating.

Debts settlement

Settling accounts for less than the total amount that you owe will hurt your credit scores. It will adversely impact your credit every time you neglect to repay a loan as originally decided. That said, the adverse effect of settlement is much smaller than the detrimental consequence of refusing to pay a loan or announcing bankruptcy at all.

Bottomline

A strong credit score will unlock the gate for a better life. By having you qualify for the better interest prices and terms while you lend money to influence how much you spend for life benefits, there might have been certain opportunities you never ever heard about. When applying for a contract, landlords may evaluate your credit scores, and even telecom companies may look at your scores before leasing your next smartphone.

Seeing how critical credit scores are for your total financial well-being, it's prudent to do whatever you can to sure yours is as high as possible. The crucial first move is reviewing your credit report and credit scores periodically. When you review your Experian credit score, you'll see a number of the variables that influence it. Firstly, focusing on certain considerations is the perfect way to continue increasing your credit score. Through leveraging your own good payment background, you can quickly improve your credit scores. It will even support you on low or small loans.

Credit repair management

There's little that a credit repair service would legitimately do for you — even deleting false information — which you couldn't manage at little to no cost of your own. And the expense of recruiting such an organization may be huge, anywhere from hundreds to thousands of dollars.

The Credit Repair Organizations Act

The Credit Repair Organizations Act is a federal law that came into force on 1st April 1997 in response to a number of consumers suffering from credit repair scams. Currently, the statute calls for credit repair company providers to:

- Companies are forbidden from taking consumer's money before the programs they offer are delivered in full.

- A formal document is specifying that the facilities to be rendered and the terms and conditions of payment to be given to customers. Within the rule, customers will withdraw from the deal within three days.

- Are prohibited from asking or suggesting that you mislead credit reporting firms about your credit accounts or change your identity to change your credit history.

- Cannot intentionally render misleading or dishonest statements regarding the programs they are capable of providing.

- Cannot request you to sign something that specifies that, under the Credit Recovery Organizations Act, you surrender your privileges. The agreement you sign is not enforceable.

You can also fix your credit

Your credit will not get a fast repair. Negative but accurate information (such as late payments and delinquencies) will remain for 7–10 years on your credit report. There are also measures you may take to continue creating a more optimistic credit profile and to increase your credit scores over time.

Check the Credit Statement

Check the credit report for a clearer view of the credit image and what lenders might expect. A few of the tips offered below, to help you understand your credit report, are:

- Know how to interpret your Report.

- Think about the fundamentals of credit reporting should you choose to know more about credit reports in general.

- You will lodge a lawsuit should you consider evidence that is inaccurate. Do remember the things you don't know on your credit report may even be possible indicators of fraudulent activity — someone acting for their own benefit to obtain credit on your behalf. Make sure you're clear about items that might be fraudulent, as opposed to items that might just be inaccurate.

Take a step to improve the payment history

One of the most important components of many FICO scoring models is your payment history. Late and missed payments will reduce your scores and may cause significant damage to public records and collections. This negative information will remain on your credit report for 7-10 years and will impact your credit scores. The size and recency of your debt are often taken into consideration in your scores. The higher your mortgage, and the more recent the missing payments will be, the lower the score will be. Having existing accounts and keeping on paying on time would nearly certainly have a good effect on your credit scores.

Keep a close eye on the credit utilization rate

Credit scoring systems typically consider how much you owe as opposed to how much credit you have, what you usually term as your credit utilization rate or your balance-to-limit ratio. It's basically the sum of all your rotating debt (such as your credit card balance) divided by the total credit available to you (or the total credit limit). High credit usage will negatively affect your credit scores. In general, maintaining the credit utilization rate below 30 percent is a safe practice. For starters, if you have a credit cap of $10,000 for all your credit cards, aim to maintain your credit card balance below $3,000 and maintain your credit utilization rate down. There are two approaches to lower the interest rates:

- Reduce debt by reimbursing the account balance
- Raise the total usable credit by increasing the current account credit cap or creating a new credit account

Although it may sound like an attractive choice to increase the credit cap, that may be a dangerous step. When you are tempted to use more credit by growing the credit cap, you may sink further into the debt. Furthermore, should you try to obtain a new credit card, an alert will surface on your credit report, and your credit score will be immediately reduced. Reducing your credit card balances and other revolving credit accounts is potentially the strongest way to increase your credit utilization rate, and therefore your credit scores. Consistent on-time payments against your debt will also help you build a positive credit history that can bring additional benefits to your credit history as well as your credit scores.

Monitor your debts and number of credit accounts

Scoring models consider how much you owe and how many different accounts you have. If you have debt across a large number of accounts, paying off some of the accounts could be beneficial if you can. Paying off the mortgage is the aim of those who have accrued a mortgage in the past, but imagine holding the account active long though you bring the balance down to zero. Holding open pay-off accounts can be a bonus in your total credit mix. You may also consider consolidating loans.

Be watchful of the credit history

Credit scoring formulas, such as those produced by FICO, also refer to the age of the oldest account and the average age of all the accounts, favoring those with longer credit histories. Only ask about your credit history before you lock an account. Leaving the account open once you have paid it off can be advantageous. Of course, if you keep accounts open and allowing credit accessibility could trigger extra spending and balance, closing the accounts could be more beneficial. Only you know all the ins and outs of your financial position, and they're specific for each guy, like thumbprints. Make sure you evaluate your situation carefully; only you know what your financial outlook can best work for.

Think multiple times before going for new credit

Opening up several credit accounts in a limited period may look dangerous to lenders and have a detrimental effect on your credit score. Once you start a new credit card account or take out a loan, remember the impact it might have on your credit scores. Remember, too, that whether you purchase a vehicle or are checking about for the right mortgage deals, the queries will be put together and classified as only one request to apply information to the credit report. Recent inquiries have a larger impact on certain widely employed rating models than older inquiries, and they occur only on the credit record after a period of 25 months.

Credit repair additional options

When the debt sounds daunting, obtaining the assistance of a reliable credit counseling provider can be worthwhile. Most are non-profit, so their services often incur low to no fees. You can study for more detail on the National Credit Counseling Foundation on finding the best credible credit counselor for you. Financial counselors will help you build a debt management program (or DMP) that can bargain on reducing the monthly payments. In certain instances, you will be liable for just one monthly contribution to the credit advisory company, which will then disburse funds to all the accounts to which you owe. Your credit report can signify accounts being charged by a Debt Management Program and not being charged as originally decided upon. Even using a Debt Management Program cannot adversely affect your credit rating if you choose to make on-time payments as negotiated to the revised terms and conditions. Additionally, you may be contemplating consolidating your loans into a personal loan or credit card swap balance. For certain situations, debt reduction loans can offer lower interest rates and lower monthly payments, as long as you qualify and stick to the conditions of the plan.

By fixing your credit swiftly

Don't panic if you make payments and your credit score is still not being revised immediately. Creditors communicate annually, typically weekly, to credit rating agencies. Based on where the creditor or lender files the changes in the month, it will take up to thirty days or longer to modify the account statuses. Typically, lenders and others use the credit score along with other financial considerations to focus on the threats they carry while lending to you. When you have negative facts regarding your credit history or a poor credit score, that may mean that you are not willing to pay off your loan as decided. They will eventually refuse you a loan or assign you higher rates and fees. When the credit report holds negative facts, it will sit there for 7-10 years. This lets lenders and others imagine the credit background easier. Although you will not be willing to alter facts from the past though, by paying the payments on time and as negotiated, you will demonstrate effective credit control going forward.

When you develop a good credit background, you are expected to increase your credit scores over time.

Analyzing credit repair ethically

In responding to this, it is important to note first that there are consumer protections written into legislation concerning how credit reporting is carried out. In other terms, credit providers are issued clear guidelines on the laws they will obey before they put adverse information on credit files. It may also come as a surprise that thirty percent of Australians who requested their credit report noticed mistakes on it in a 2013 survey conducted by the Australian Information Commissioner and that only 60 percent of respondents who identified mistakes had them corrected. Around this stage, it needs to be mentioned that the credit reports include 'small M' errors and 'capital M' errors. 'Minor M' mistakes involve details included on your credit reports, such as an erroneous birth date, name spelling or address, or a credit page not yours. Credit repair companies don't fix these 'small M' errors at a fee because, frankly, you can do it yourself. No one ever gets in touch with a credit repair company to get the correct spelling of their name or patch an incorrect address. Credit repair companies will be contacted regarding 'capital M' errors. Typically, the customer goes to a broker to arrange loans for a house or other property, and when the credit file is evaluated, the broker will not be able to move forward with applying for a loan at the best interest rate because the adverse listings (defaults, rulings, writs, etc.) hinder the procedure. This is when credit repair applications are provided to the customer. The customer may have a listing that he didn't know about, or he knew about it, so he felt the method was unreasonable leading up to the release. Credit repair companies ask the client and credit company for clarification about the circumstances leading up to unfavorable listings and require credit providers to show that they have met the regulations since the listing was made. And with so many credit reporting errors being reported by the Information Commissioner Report, why would some brokers always believe credit repair is immoral, and the credit reporting system is disturbing? Instead, maybe they should extend the word 'unethical' to anyone that positions listings on credit reports that contravene the legislation. Consequently, credit repair firms can not erase correctly placed credit file information. It is only as plain as this. Recording these details is crucial and useful to credit companies when evaluating prospective borrowers and the loan products they may be selling them. Nobody is seeking to disrupt fair credit reporting. All credit restoration firms do is delete information that is wrongly put. In fact, an increasing number of people seem to be disagreeing with the credit recovery method. Some claim it's not appropriate to challenge an object you think is right. For starters, during difficult times a couple of years ago, you skipped two car payments, and today you seek to buy a house. Your credit score has to go up 80 points to gain funding. You agree to go on with a credit restoration company because at that stage; there are few other choices. This is the splitting moment for people. Some want the best technically possible results, and others claim I don't want to try to remove a negative mark that I know is true. Here are two items you need to learn about it:

- There's nothing to keep you from using a credit repair program and opting not to contest things that you know are true.

- The term used for a justification in the Fair Credit Reporting Act is "exact." Accuracy in the field of credit reporting demands that the creditor maintain its interest with your credit profile for the entire time the object has an effect on your credit score. If the borrower loses interest or fails to respond, otherwise the credit report removes the paper.

Section 609 Dispute Letter

A 609 Dispute Letter is also advertised as a confidential or legitimate backdoor for financial restoration that requires credit rating companies to delete any derogatory details on the credit records. This helps to improve the credit score. Section 609 applies to a provision of the Fair Credit Reporting Act (FCRA) that recognizes the ability to obtain copies of your own credit reports and related material found on your credit reports. Yes, the FCRA contains a large deal of vocabulary that can memorize the ability to challenge the facts contained on the credit reports. Yet it's in Statute section 611, rather than section 609. We also have the freedom to challenge facts due to section 611, which we consider to be inaccurate or unverifiable. So, if the knowledge at question cannot be checked or validated, then it must be excluded.

CHAPTER 4: Writing a Dispute Letter

Consumers normally send grievance letters to big credit reporting agencies if they think something is wrong with their credit report. This can happen if they have applied for a loan or other form of credit and they have been informed by the lender that they have been denied due to information in their credit report. When they search their credit report and discover accounts they don't remember; it can also happen. A dispute letter's practical effect is it causes the credit reporting agency to investigate and correct any alleged error. Therefore, if the credit reporting information is accurate and verifiable, then chances are it will remain on your credit reports. Your letter style doesn't alter the reality. You'll be relieved to know that in many cases, a 609 letter does absolutely work. Consumers appear to have a lot of trouble as part of a credit recovery phase with 609 notes, which may be how often borrowers collect documents electronically without having all the correct documentation and reports they are expected to provide. If you have worked on repairing your credit and boosting your credit score and your standard disputes have not worked, a letter of 609 may just be the solution you need. And if you've only one and two stubborn things you won't get rid of, that might be the right way to do it.

Interpretation of Section 609 of the FCRA

Several stipulations put out by the FCRA are developed to prevent identity fraud, and one of them is Section 609. Section 609 aims to make it harder for people to get credit data about others. Section 609 of the FCRA notes that all users have the ability to request the release of all details in their accounts, the origin of the details, and the identity of any individual who has received the credit report. And if any of such facts are not checked by the credit rating

service, they will delete the derogatory label on the credit report. In other terms, in order to disclose adverse behavior lawfully, creditors have to keep highly trustworthy and detailed accounts on all of their dealings with customers.

What does a 609-credit dispute letter contain?

You may be able to get negative items deleted from your credit report based on Section 609, and many others have been popular in the process, increasing their credit score. The fundamental process includes writing a letter requesting confirmation of all the data in your file in the hope that something was not properly documented.

If, in fact, the creditor failed to properly document something, they have no official choice but to eliminate that negative thing from your credit report.

Ways to contest an error on the credit report

You begin by disputing one thing directly with the credit reporting offices. Every credit bureau has a way to challenge all of your credit products, and you can do so electronically if you want, or by sending them a letter, you can file it in person. Often after your first argument, a credit reporting organization may erase an object, so you will often be needed to follow up with additional paperwork. For instance, if an object involves a flaw in the ledger, you may require to provide receipts or other documentation explaining why you think it's incorrect.

The obligation of credit bureaus

Most accountability for honest reports, in turn, rests with the credit management offices, due to which the legal cycle continues for them much of the time. Credit rating services are allowed to provide only truthful and verifiable details on the credit report, according to the FCRA. It ensures that if the investors don't get appropriate answers from the credit office, they will be obliged to delete all derogatory things on the credit sheet.

What 609 letters fail to achieve?

It's essential to know that while a 609 letter may help with repairing your credit, it doesn't help you with your debt. Whether it's a legal loan otherwise, you do have an obligation to pay it off. Another factor you should be mindful of is that if the creditor were still willing to check the facts regarding the credit report in query, a deleted object might be reinserted. Therefore, though credit monitoring offices can withdraw an object if a creditor refuses to reply within thirty days, they do have the ability to send their proof later. And last but not least, if a creditor has sold your bank account to a balance settlement service, you may see the similar debt crop up again from another company. This can occur if you continue to be delinquent with the bank account you still owe cash on. And that may not really be the end of things, only because you effectively contest an object with the initial creditor. When that occurs, otherwise, you may have to go into the fight with the payment agency again and attempt and have them excluded as well.

How to write an effective dispute letter?

If you send a credit claim letter to a credit office, you first need to locate your credit report — this can be a bigger task than it seems, particularly since the credit office in question may have reported about almost everybody in the world reporting on it. You will need to provide detail on the mistake after you have found the submission, as well as a clarification as to why you are disputing the object. Eventually, the payment claim letter should include a request to remove the object from the credit report to the credit bureau.

It should have what it needs to make a decision on your case by providing the bureau the necessary information. Here's what to include.

- Updated date

- The particulars (name, contact information, date of birth, and account number)

- Contact information for the Credit office

- A brief description of the mistake (no need for a long and complicated tale to regale them)

- Any documentation you might have that can help prove your point, like payment histories or court documents (make sure to mention in the letter why you submitted them)

- Notes on what you need the credit office to do (re-examine and delete the element from your report)

- A duplicate of the credit report labeled with a mistake

- A scanned copy of your Government ID (such as your driver's license) and a bill or other paper showing your identity

Here are just a few samples of arguable products.

- Collections

- Late payments

- Bankruptcies are not stopped until 7 to 10 years

- Pre-closures not lifted until seven years

Bottomline

609 Dispute letters are a perfect place to theoretically clear out a few derogatory things that you would not have been able to delete earlier from your credit report. Even if these things are yours, creditors have to register them properly and be prepared to show them.

But bear in mind that traditional disputes over credit reporting are fine, to begin with since you may initially find some inaccuracies that need to be addressed. But these 609 letters are yet another tool in your arsenal on your road to a better score, although they don't do the trick.

CHAPTER 5: Rebuilding your Credit after Critical Life Events

There are options to monitor, secure and repair the credit ratings after big live incidents such as marriage, divorce or a spouse's death. Better credit will make the financial conditions in other lives smoother and less stressful. For example, you can get authorized for a loan or automatic loan with good credit and possibly be eligible for the decent interest rates and conditions available. A decent credit record will also influence how much premiums you pay and how a gas provider calls for little to no payment when you start a business.

Techniques for rebuilding credit

When you have committed financial errors in the history, your credit ratings might not be as good as you would like. Although you may not be able to erase such past derogatory things from your credit report immediately because they are correct, you should take action to create a more optimistic background profile beginning today to boost your financial growth.

Factors Influencing Credit Scores

Several factors can have an impact on credit scores. Some common credit scoring factors are:

History of Payment

It's data that keeps track of the on-time payment along with late or skipped payments.

Credit utilization ratio

It measures the overall amount of credit you have reserved to the amount of credit you're already using.

Total debt

It refers to the gross liability, which involves credit cards, deposits, collections, as well as other credit accounts.

Mix

It is the type of credit accounts that you are using.

Age

It defines the age of your credit accounts.

Hard inquiries

Hard inquiries are associated with your current applications for the latest credit.

People records

Those are tax documents or federal trial decisions. The only way to learn what variables influence the credit ratings is to browse at them regularly. It should allow you to get a rundown of the variables of credit performance that most affect its ranking. If you are attempting to enhance your credit scores, you need to consider first addressing those factors. Also, monitor your credit frequently-to have a good eye on your score-your credit report information and your growth over time.

Take wise steps for rebuilding the credit

If you have poorer credit scores than you would like, realize that change starts with you! The steps you take to adjust your credit actions are normally reflected in your credit scores as positive updates over a period because all the steps you take when it comes to credit are the data that goes into your scores.

Bills Payment on Time

To stop any derogatory feedback about your credit report, stick to the following:

- Pay the bills on schedule every month.

- When you have any previous balances due, carry the existing accounts with you and make deposits on schedule.

- Try setting up recurring transfers or bill alerts to better guarantee the bill is never late.

Give due consideration to your Credit Utilization Ratio

One likes their payment cards to max up, so investors do not want to see bank reports that seem maxed-out either. Your credit use ratio measures the overall amount of credit that you have, depending on credit card guidelines, to the sum of credit that you currently utilize (your balance). Many specialists warn you to maintain it below 30 percent. You will lower the credit usage level through:

- Paying off debt from credit card

- Maintaining small to negative credit card balances

- Be vigilant when clearing accounts. When you shut down an account, you decrease your total credit number, which in effect influences your credit usage ratio

Go for a secured account

Opening a safe account, such as a secured credit card, will help you establish a good financial background which can be a useful option if you're having difficulty obtaining standard credit or credit card approvals. You invest cash into an account with a safe loan as leverage and only repay a portion of the amount for credit. The use of a protected credit account is disclosed to credit agencies, and a positive payment record helps in building your reputation when you pay your monthly bill. Opening a new account would also build a hard investigation with the study-so be sure this is something you are sparingly doing.

Seek help from friends and family

Your friends and family may be prepared to support you in developing your reputation. You will do it in a variety of forms, including:

- Enable you to become a registered recipient with another credit card

- Access your Mutual Account

- Act as a co-signer to help you obtain a loan that you may not otherwise apply for

Be wary of new credit

Opening, or even simply applying for, new credit card accounts can change your credit **scores**. Improving the quantity of credit, you have at your fingertips will increase your ratio of **credit** utilization, but only if you have the will to pay your bills every month. What's more, any credit card transaction you create will show on your credit report as a strict inquiry, and so many strict inquiries in a small-time can have a detrimental effect on your credit scores. A lender may also see various applications for credit cards within a small time period and view that as an indication you are in hot financial water and use credit to survive above your requirements. Lenders usually want to make confident that you are not at risk of financially

overextending yourself until deciding to lend additional

credit.

Free Credit Score

Knowing your FICO ® Score * is really essential, particularly when you're contemplating making a major purchase. You will need to consider whether your FICO ® Score benefits or hurts, like your payment background, how much credit you use, and other variables that affect your total ranking. Throughout fact, strong credit ratings are the ticket toward favorable mortgage interest rates, vehicles, credit card deals, insurance premiums and more. Good ratings are worth the investment because they will save you so much. Your credit report says potential lenders just how responsible you have been in the earlier period with credit. Legally, creditors should ask for this checklist to decide how dangerous it is to give to you.

Your credit background shows the specifics of the previous loan accounts and existing ones. It also records your credit report any time you or a partner demands it, as well as times when your loans have been transferred to a collection group. Also included are financial matters that are a portion of the public data, such as foreclosures and bankruptcies. Your credit score is a figure which is the credit value. Scores can also be represented as credit rankings, and at times as FICO ® Scores, produced by Fair Isaac Company and typically ranges from 300 - 850.

Responsibility is the key

It is critical above all that credit be used responsibly. A strong financial history and credit score may be the difference in purchasing a house, owning a vehicle or paying for college. Managing your credit report proactively is a smart opportunity to stay in charge of your accounts and eventually accomplish your goals.

Where To Get Your FICO® Scores

Over 90 percent of U.S. lending decisions use FICO ® Scores. There are lots of "check ratings" accessible to customers, and it's crucial to consider what score you receive and how often borrowers use it or not using it — so it's more critical than ever to make sure you recognize your FICO ® rating.

Authorized FICO® Score Retailers

Buy your FICO ® Scores directly from an accredited FICO ® Score dealer to ensure that you have your FICO ® Scores — not any other credit score form. They don't offer FICO ® Scores if they're not mentioned. Only Equifax ® products containing a specific FICO ® Score are supplied with FICO ® Scores, including the Credit Score Watch ® product and the Score Power ® product. Many Equifax ® products may include credit scores, not FICO ® Ratings.

FICO® Score Open Access Program

FICO ® Score Easy Access is a service that helps teach customers about FICO ® Scores and expands exposure to FICO ® Scores for users. FICO partners with more than 200 financial companies to provide their customers with completely free exposure to the FICO ® Ratings they use to monitor credit accounts. Whether your branch, credit card processor, auto lender or mortgage service company invests in FICO ® Score Easy Access, you can access your FICO ® Scores free of charge along with the key variables that impact your ratings.

FICO® Score Open Access for Credit and Financial Counseling Program

FICO ® Score Open Access for Credit and Financial

Counseling enables providers of credit and financial counseling to share the FICO ® Scores with their clients. The software was primarily developed by credit and financial counselors to improve customer awareness of FICO Ratings and their role in day-to-day financial decision-making. More than 100 therapy agencies are involved, and this service has exchanged more than 250,000 credit ratings with customers.

Find out about your Credit Scores for Free

You don't have to compensate for seeing all of your credit histories. The credit report presents an almost full record of the credit history. Many of the financial requests are based on the data in your credit report, whether directly or indirectly. For example, you need to be sure that the information on your credit report is correct. It's suggested that you verify your credit report once a year at least to make sure no errors occur. The more often the credit report is reviewed, the healthier. Luckily there are several ways to free test your credit report. The good free credit reports don't ask for sign-up credit card data and can be easily accessible online. When checking out your free credit report, make sure that you access a safe website and understand any fine printing on the site. The best free credit reports which are best recommended to use are given below.

AnnualCreditReport.com-The Best Free Option

Federal legislation enacted in 2003 giving every user the right to a free audit from all credit reporting organizations every year. AnnualCreditReport.com is the online platform that helps any user to view their Federal Law providing free credit report. This is the only platform that permits you to view, at no expense, each of your credit records from all three main credit agencies, including Experian, Equifax, and TransUnion. Via AnnualCreditReport.com, you will get one annual credit report every twelve months without signing up, developing an account or enrolling your credit card details. Credit reports can be accessed as a File, or you can pay to have your credit reports sent to you. The drawback is that you submit a complete credit report which is not user-friendly written. The credit reports can be hundreds of pages overall, depending on the size of the credit record and the number of accounts you've had. For the AnnualCreditReport.com credit report, you won't get a credit score.

Credit Karma for Credit Monitoring

Since 2006, Credit Karma has combined with 2 of the big credit agencies —TransUnion and Equifax — to deliver an annual credit check. Considering that you should run two of the big credit records, AnnualCreditReport.com is the next safest choice. While you'll need to make an account to use Good Karma, you don't need to insert credit card data or recall terminating any free subscription. By signing into your account either directly from your net browser or via their mobile application, you can view your credit reports at any time. The record on the credit report is modified as often as once a week, allowing you continued access to improvements in your credit info. You will have access to information regarding your credit report, along with a summary of the factors currently leading to your credit count. Credit Karma also uses the free credit report info to view loan deals and the credit card you may apply for depending on your credit standing. If you're not on the marketplace for a new credit card or loan program, you don't have to take advantage of those deals.

Credit Sesame

Credit Sesame should include details regarding your TransUnion credit report along with the variables that most impact your score. Like Credit Luck, you sign up by making an account, but the payment card details do not have to be entered. Your subscription would give you an entree to a monthly refresh of your credit records after you have established an account. However, you may access your account at any time. You will also have links to your TransUnion credit record online or via the Credit Sesame smartphone app, in addition to the statistics on the TransUnion credit card. Reviewing your records also offers you a sense of where your reputation stands and how your ranking needs to be changed. Credit Sesame examines the personal history to suggest payment cards, investments and other financial items, so you don't have to qualify for a new loan if you're not on the marketplace.

NerdWallet

Register with NerdWallet and have links to your TransUnion credit card for free. Your credit report particulars are updated regularly with Nerdwallet, but you can sign in to review your credit report info at any time. Additionally, to the free credit report, you will now access the VantageScore 3.0 depending on the knowledge on the TransUnion credit card. Additionally, the credit report is changed regularly. It is relatively easy to sign. You can make use of your current Google account and build your account, and you only need to enter the last 4 digits of your Security. Optionally, you can open the Nerdwallet iOS app to track your credit score and other facets of your assets instantly and conveniently when you're on the move.

Bankrate for Personalized Analysis

Bankrate offers you complete, direct access to TransUnion information regarding your credit score in a special interface that is simpler to interpret than many other credit report providers. In a linear chart, Bankrate sets out your credit history details to demonstrate how the credit rating has improved over time. You should take a glance at your financial background and find important factors that may have affected your score-for better or worse. If the credit report details improve, you will consider if such adjustments may have affected the credit score and also identify things in your credit report that could suggest a risk for fraud. You'll always get a free credit score, combined with your free credit survey and your performance review. The insights should help you understand the factors that influence your credit score, see whether your credit score is trending up or down, and learn how your financial practices can affect your credit score.

CreditWise for Improving Credit

You can test your TransUnion credit score and credit report via CreditWise, a Capital One credit score and credit report tool. Credit Wise is accessible free of charge, even to those who aren't Capital One clients. It's easy and simple to sign up for. You will not have to submit any credit card details, there is no free trial subscription to cancel, and your credit details are updated weekly.

WalletHub for daily Updates

The details on the credit report will alter periodically when the creditors submit reports to the credit offices. Weekly or weekly notifications may leave the credit report information a little out of reach. WalletHub is the only platform that offers the full credit score history with free email alerts, along with a rundown of significant improvements to the credit record. You would have the latest current details from your TransUnion credit report and helps you to respond quickly on your credit report for adjustments or suspicious behavior. WalletHub also offers personalized credit recommendations directly focused on your credit records.

Why should one check a credit report?

Blunders also happen. Indeed, the Federal Trade Commission reports that at least 1 in 5 customers has one error in their credit report. These mistakes can impact your skill to gain approvals or can make you pay high costs when approved. The best way to ensure that the credit report includes the correct details is by regular analysis of the reports.

Are Free Credit Reports Worthwhile?

Buying your credit reports can be costly, particularly if you choose to check your credit report several times a year. Log in with a free credit report helps you to live without the big price tag and stay on top of your score. And, for a detailed peek at your history through the three main credit bureaus, you can utilize a more free credit report facility at a time. Testing your free credit report will be a clear indication of where your credit is and how your report needs to be changed. In addition to certain requirements, lenders such as credit card firms, banks and car dealerships offering auto loans use credit scores to determine whether to accept you for credit. Knowing your credit score will help you to plan and avoid surprises such as adverse conditions or even denials when applying for a loan or other form of credit. Credit scores modify continuously. If you note your scores are down, there might be a number of explanations for such changes. For instance, if you have a late or missing payment or have just qualified for a new loan or credit card, the score may have fallen. Certain potential explanations involve expanded usage of credit, the closing of an account or a fresh derogatory label on the record. Checking your free credit score can help you narrow down the reasons behind the dropping of your credit score.

CHAPTER 6: Critical Information on Credit Scores

When you don't have a loan background, beginning to build up your credit may be a bit of a struggle. You may not have adequate credit background to earn a credit score. There are many ways to set up credit according to your age. You may need a career, so you may need to open a credit card with a co-signer that has credit set up. Some choices include insured credit cards (that include a deposit), store credit cards, and credit cards for schools. As long as you have a loan or credit card linked to your account, credit agencies can start developing your credit report. When you use your credit wisely, you can earn access to more of it over time. If you're under the age of twenty, you'll need to have a co-signer or be able to prove that you have a sufficient source of income to pay back the extra loan. A parent who cosigns a credit card for conscientious usage (or adds you as an authorized user to one of their accounts) makes way for you to help build a good credit background. For others, negotiating with the bank or credit union to open an account with a limited credit limit to get you going might be the best way to establish credit. Opening a secured credit card is another means of having the credit building going. Therefore, a good credit background (and scores) will be within your control, with patience and proper account management.

Essential Credit Score Facts

Given below are some important facts relevant to credit score:

Credit Reports and Credit History

Credit scores are not made part of credit records. Moreover, credit history does not hold records of your credit score. Your credit score can only be determined after requesting the credit score. Your credit score can change over time, depending on your credit history — including late payments, amount of debt available, etc.

Joint Accounts

Joint funds are designed to support people who cannot qualify for a credit on their own. The specific account holders, guarantors, and/or cosigners are liable for repaying the loan with joint accounts. The shared record with both account holders shows on the credit report, along with the payment background. The joint account will help create good credibility when all the payments are made on time. When anyone defaults on fees, though, the joint account managers can have the error in their own credit records. Based on the extent of late payments and negative information, the credit ratings of both may be negatively affected.

There are separate credit reports for couples

Each partner gets their own credit report, even after marriage. The credit history of each person includes only the information which is recorded on their behalf. If the lenders report their records under the current name, Experian can compare them to the established background and keep checking them, but only with the names connected with the account.

Joint accounts appear on both credit reports

Therefore, the accounts and credit history of your partner, including bankruptcy, would not be applied to your credit record before the marriage until you get married and until your name is attached to them. Your credit data will not be applied to the record either-unless you apply it to the records as a joint partner. Your spouse would profit from being a joint account holder on your accounts as his credit report will have the favorable payment background applied. It may be useful since you are likely to choose to apply for shared loans that would require you to qualify for both your salary and credit records, such as an auto loan, and the vehicle title will appear in each of your names. Marriage is a relationship, so you should work together to rebuild the imperfect credit past, but it doesn't mean that by doing that, you have to destroy your credit history.

Know how to enhance your credit score by 100 points in just 30 days

You can improve credit scores by as much as 100 points in 30 days through the following steps:

You need to get a copy of the personal credit report and scores

You may need to review your credit report before you begin research on your credit. Finding out the FICO score for all three credit bureaus is always a good idea.

Find the negative accounts

Finally, after having your credit score, go over it to show negative-status

accounts. You would still need to identify some late fees, fraud reports, or something similar and requests for credit.

Make sure your personal information, including your address, your employer and your phone number, is accurate. You should concentrate on late fees, fraud reports, credit inquiries and past or current contact inaccuracies.

Pay off credit card balances

Your credit usage ratio is the sum of the credit card balance compared to the credit cap. It is important to hold the ratio below 15 percent. Your credit usage ratio affects your FICO score by a huge 30 percent amount. Just your payment background (30 percent) has a larger effect on your credit ranking overall. When you have a heavy balance on your credit card otherwise your credit performance would fail. Fund your credit card balances to zero or as close to zero as you can to rising the credit usage levels to the lowest level to improve the FICO ratings.

Get in touch with collection agencies

If you have tiny accounts or unpaid payment bills, you can contact the payment agent. Tell them you'd like to do a remove fee. Pay-for-delete is exactly as it looks like, you pay the due balance, and they erase the derogatory record completely from your credit report. You will require letters from the collection department "pay for erasing" in a paper stating they plan to remove the transaction completely from your record if you reimburse the sum decided upon. You will be allowed to resolve the debt for less than you owe in certain situations, but others would require you to compensate in full if they erase it from the payment history.

Avoid paying for the collection account

A collection account is a collection account, which has the same impact on the credit record, irrespective of whether it is a zero balance or a balance of $20,000. Don't bill collecting accounts without a letter "bill for erasing." Compensation for loss is an offer to compensate the unpaid balance if the settlement firm deletes the payment completely from the credit sheet. The only way that can boost credit ratings is to get items deleted from the record like they were never present in the first place. When a lender claims they're going to mark it as charged but can't erase it, don't reimburse it if the credit score isn't going to change.

Disputing the negative information will also be advantageous

Unless the lender is unable to check the account authenticity, late payment, balance, or something you have contested, otherwise, they can withdraw the object. In a nutshell, this is credit restoration. A case may also be lodged electronically or via fax.

Try to get late payments removed

When you have an account or late payment with the initial trustee, you will realize that a letter of goodwill would no longer function. It is against the Credit Bureau's arrangement with borrowers to delete a derogatory object as a gesture of kindness or for some other excuse that it is wrong. Alternatively, call the trustee first to inform them you believe the late charge is wrong. Most certainly, they would have their credit monitoring department reviewing the commodity. If this doesn't succeed, you might start quarreling with the three big credit monitoring agencies. You will see your credit score improved by 70-80 points in a month if you fail to have late payments dropped.

Disputing credit inquiries will also help

Strong investigations live twenty-four months on the account sheet. We would affect twelve months on your credit report. But, on your credit record, you can challenge hard inquiries and get them dropped. For the challenge, queries contact the payment bureaus. The lender will check that you have approved them to take out the loan. This is a perfect, fast way to catch up on credit scores.

Get yourself added as an authorized user

An authenticated user indicates you are entitled to access the account using your credit card. Authorized users to make transactions that have their own card with their name on it. Registered users are not the sole owners of the account, though. When the password falls to default, the registered users would be responsible. Authorized consumers often enjoy the rewards of a successful payment background favorable record. Verify that the account you are linking to is in good standing. When the lender announces your current account status, all payment data should appear on the sheet. This will boost several points in your credit score and help create confidence for others without FICO ratings. Be sure that you are allowing financially stable individuals who you know well to sign in as an approved person; it can be very helpful to easily improve your credit score.

Things the credit bureaus want to keep undisclosed

Here are some things the credit bureaus don't want you to know about how they work.

Impact on your life

Check offices not only monitor personal credit records but also retain a broad variety of other pieces of details, such as past addresses and records of work. This may be collected by lenders (at a premium-selling customer details is a big source of income for credit offices) and used to determine whether to grant a loan or not and at what interest rate. Such documents may even hinder the decision to find a new apartment (before considering an application, many landlords check at the background history) or even affect a work application since federal legislation requires employees to request credit files on employment applicants. Approximately 47 percent of managers agree that they did so before hiring new workers.

Accurate reporting

Given the tremendous effect of a disappointing study, you might be expecting that intense action will be taken to ensure consistency in results. That is not necessarily the case, though. A Federal Trade Commission analysis has reported mistakes in credit reports by 1 in 5 customers.

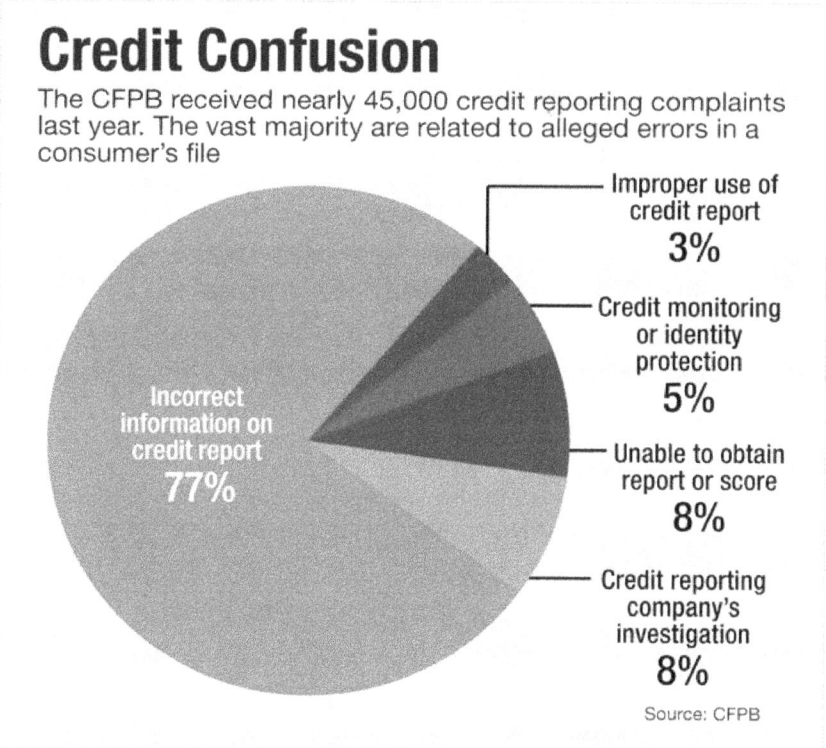

Credit Confusion

The CFPB received nearly 45,000 credit reporting complaints last year. The vast majority are related to alleged errors in a consumer's file

Improper use of
credit report
3%

Credit monitoring
or identity
protection
5%

Incorrect
information on
credit report
77%

Unable to obtain
report or score
8%

Credit reporting
company's
investigation
8%

Source: CFPB

The map above illustrates the key explanations provided to the Consumer Financial Security Bureau in 2014 for concerns regarding consumer credit reports. As you can see, they were primarily linked to inaccurate credit reporting details. Another cause of concern applies to the inquiry by the credit reporting service. Many borrowers who decide to contest a lawsuit investigation's conclusions will face a long struggle to appeal the ruling, with some of such lawsuits extending up to 10 years. A 2011 report sponsored by the credit industry found that 95 percent of conflicts are resolved to the benefit of the customer. Credit bureaus and certain organizations may often render the failure to receive a receipt or ranking worse. Any of those would offer their credit report to a creditor for a small charge. When you want to do so, test carefully which score you really receive. For certain instances, it could be an 'educational ranking' and is not likely to be the same as the performance a lender gives. While applying for loans, this will create problems that contribute to excessively high-interest rates.

Checking your credit report

To see that they are correct, it is highly advised to have your own credit reports when applying for loans or a career. You are allowed to appeal it under the 'Secure Credit Reporting Act' if you review the record and notice an error or a derogatory thing that can impact the credit score.

The terms of the Act

You are eligible to challenge incorrect results at any point on your credit sheet. When questioned on an item, the credit bureau shall examine the matter free of charge within the duration of 30 days unless notice of delay is issued. Every element challenged in this manner must either be checked by the creditor with written evidence or, if a mistake is detected, promptly fixed or removed.

When the credit bureau and trustee are unwilling or reluctant to validate the case finding within 30 days, the object will be deleted from the credit report. If the inquiry by the creditor considers a contested object to be correct, you have the option to make your own Customer Complaint in the case.

Further possibilities

Accurate; however, misleading facts on the credit report will usually not be contested. These details will stay seven years on the record (10 for bankruptcies).

If this detail persists beyond this stage in your record, you are allowed to challenge this with the credit bureaus and apply for it to be deleted.

Avoid the bad credit with the right mindset

A perspective towards money is an overarching mentality you have about your finances. It influences every day the way you make important financial choices. It will significantly affect your potential to attain your goals. If you shift your perspective on income, you continue to make smarter choices on how problems can be solved. The influence of constructive thought does indeed apply in this situation.

Features of a bad money mindset

Your attitude towards money is like moral fatigue-it pushes you to act. If you have a positive mentality about finances, you are more likely to be confident and take the measures you need to take to be effective. On the other hand, negativity is generating emotions that prevent action:

- Fear or intimidation
- Defeatism
- Procrastination

It's harder to see the way ahead as you shift your attitude towards money and concentrate on the benefits of what you should achieve. A fresh outlook on money will help you easily reach your goals. So how do you build a positive mentality on money?

Qualities of a positive money mindset

Once you accept financial positivity, you begin to understand that no issue is insurmountable. This will be reduced if you have $5,000 in interest or $50,000. Your credit score maybe 500, but there is no loan limit that would last forever.

When you have a good attitude regarding finances, instead of seeing roadblocks, you start searching for possibilities and realize that any financial problem is fixable. The secret to success is to resolve negative feelings, to concentrate on the optimistic.

How to get rid of collection calls and creditor harassment

Given below are helpful steps to stop collection calls and creditor harassment:

Identify Your Debts

Take note of all the payment cards, credit lines and loans to figure out which ones you're late on. Check back at the credit history to see which transactions have been turned at or been overdue to a collection agent. When the loan is not yours because you have already paid it back, let the payment agent and credit monitoring services know so that any false records will be deleted from your record. Thereafter you do not accept phone calls (if you do, you should refer the collector to the province's consumer protection authority). Yet if you claim the unpaid loans, you'll need to look after them.

Know Your Rights

Aggressive debt collectors may be threatening, but the information is your strongest security-get familiar with your privileges, and you realize when they cross the mark.

Collection companies are authorized by statute to notify you about any unpaid debts you owe. They cannot use profanity, make threats or lose their patience as they speak. Debt creditors have to comply with fixed hours and procedures. It covers how many days within a day or a week they should email you, whether they can call you, and whether they can reach your boss at all. Look closely at the letters that you receive — they may seem like formal legal papers or legal instructions to settle your debts. This, too, is unconstitutional.

Take Action

When the offensive phone calls are irrational, take action to avoid them finding successful means to connect with borrowers and enforcement companies on their tracks. Test to ensure you are accredited to the collection service that is calling you. When they are illegal and have broken the rules, refer them to the authority in charge of consumer safety. Depending on what has occurred and whether they become a serial abuser, it is up to them to cancel a collector's license. Finally, you will avoid the irritating phone calls by submitting a formal request that debt collectors just speak with you in person.

Conclusion

When applying for credit cards and loans, having a good credit history can help you get better terms as well as conditions. You'll benefit from lower interest rates, which will save you money in the long run. Maintaining low balances as well as credit limits on cards can help you establish and operate good credit. Keep in mind that having a lot of debt and having a lot of credit limits can hurt your credit score. You can also help your credit score by avoiding opening new credit card accounts that you don't require. If you've had credit problems in the past, you'll need to rebuild your credit history. Create new accounts and make good use of them. You have to ensure that you pay them back in a timely manner. You should not be afraid to use accounts that you've had for a long time. Keep an established account with a long record of on-time payments if you want to keep your credit score high. You should always be thinking about the future. It is simply because accounts can stay on the credit report for a maximum of seven years. You really should avoid having a bad credit score. Carrying a lot of debt, making late payments, and missing payments can all hurt your credit. Paying only the minimum amount due on bills like cell phones, credit cards, student loans, and car loans can also contribute to poor credit. Bad credit can have far-reaching negative implications for your credit score. It's possible that you'll be turned down for credit. If your credit is extremely bad, you may be unable to obtain any type of loan, even at exorbitant interest rates. It's also possible that you'll miss out on job opportunities. It's because many employers run credit checks on potential employees before they hire them. Your housing choices become limited or restricted as well. Many landlords will not let you sign a lease till they have run your credit report. As a result of your poor credit, you will pay higher interest rates on loans and credit cards. Similarly, you will pay higher insurance premiums for your car, health, rental, and homeowners' insurance. The interest ratio is among the costs associated with lending money, and it is often directly related to the credit score. You'll almost qualify for the good interest rates and pay lower finance rates on credit card balances as well as loans if you have a good credit score. The less interest you pay, the faster you'll be able to pay off your debt and have more money for other things. Borrowers with a weak credit history are often hesitant to apply for a new credit card as well as a loan because they have previously been denied. Because lenders take into account other factors such as your debt and income, having a nice credit score isn't a guarantee of approval. A good credit score, on the other hand, increases the likelihood of getting new credit. Alternatively, you can confidently ask for a loan or a credit card. With a great credit score, you can get a better interest percentage on a credit card or even a new loan. If you want more negotiating leverage, you can use other appealing offers based on the credit score that you've received from other companies. Creditors are highly improbable to budge on loan terms if you have a low credit score, and you won't have any credit offers as well as options. An exceptional credit score is something to be proud of because of the numerous benefits it provides, especially if you've worked hard to improve your credit score from bad to good. Moreover, if you've never had a bad credit score before, keep doing what you can to keep it that way.

www.ingramcontent.com/pod-product-compliance
Lightning Source LLC
Chambersburg PA
CBHW050125240326
41458CB00122B/1419